- As Time Goes By -
Beachmere Memories
2026
Calendar & Journal

Author and Photographer: Chris Sutton

Title: As Time Goes By - Beachmere Memories 2026

Subtitle: Calendar & Journal

Publisher: M.C. Sutton Publications
139/218 Bishop Rd, Beachmere, 4510

ISBN: 978-0-646-72182-8

Dedication

For my friends and neighbours, and our lovely community. You make life in our little town so good.

Record the memories of each month spent in this super chill little town at the mouth of the Caboolture River.

Share the memories you record with your children and grandchildren when they ask what your life was like in 2026.

Or, give each of your children and grandchildren their own book, so that they too can record their memories of 2026, and bring them out in 10, 20, 50 years time to share with future generations.

January

Sun	Mon	Tues	Wed	Thurs	Fri	Sat
				1	2	3
4	5	6	7	8	9	10
11	12	13	14	15	16	17
18	19	20	21	22	23	24
25	26 AUSTRALIA DAY	27	28	29	30	31

The off-leash dog area at the mouth of the Caboolture River is an excellent place to exercise your dogs in January. There's plenty of shade and at low tide, a wide stretch of rippled sand and small lagoons where dogs of all sizes can run, play and cool off.

Qld School Holidays

Public Holidays

Qld/Brisbane

Appointments

_____
_____
_____
_____
_____
_____
_____
_____
_____
_____
_____
_____
_____
_____
_____
_____
_____
_____
_____
_____

This month's memories

_____
_____
_____
_____
_____
_____
_____
_____
_____
_____
_____
_____
_____
_____
_____
_____
_____
_____
_____
_____
_____

February

Sun	Mon	Tues	Wed	Thurs	Fri	Sat
1	2	3	4	5	6	7
8	9	10	11	12	13	14
15	16	17	18	19	20	21
22	23	24	25	26	27	28

In February, the Lilly Pilly blooms and the bees are busy making honey. You'll hear their loud buzzing and see all sizes and shapes of native and domesticated bees. If you are really lucky you may find a solitary carpenter bee taking leaves back to her hole in a Lilliy Pilly branch.

Qld School Holidays   Public Holidays   Qld /Brisbane

Appointments

_____
_____
_____
_____
_____
_____
_____
_____
_____
_____
_____
_____
_____
_____
_____
_____
_____
_____

This month's memories

_____
_____
_____
_____
_____
_____
_____
_____
_____
_____
_____
_____
_____
_____
_____
_____
_____
_____
_____

March

Sun	Mon	Tues	Wed	Thurs	Fri	Sat
1	2	3	4	5	6	7
8	9	10	11	12	13	14
15	16	17	18	19	20	21
22	23	24	25	26	27	28
29	30	31				

Beachmere is blessed with a myriad of bird species thanks to its rich natural environment.In March, the bush is ablaze with Melaleuca blossoms, and alive with the chattering and squawking of Rainbow Lorikeets as they make the most of the nectar flow.

Qld School Holidays

Public Holidays

Qld /Brisbane

Appointments

_____
_____
_____
_____
_____
_____
_____
_____
_____
_____
_____
_____
_____
_____
_____
_____
_____
_____
_____

This month's memories

_____
_____
_____
_____
_____
_____
_____
_____
_____
_____
_____
_____
_____
_____
_____
_____
_____
_____
_____
_____
_____

April

Sun	Mon	Tues	Wed	Thurs	Fri	Sat
					EASTER	
			1	2	3	4
EASTER						
5	6	7	8	9	10	11
12	13	14	15	16	17	18
					ANZAC DAY	
19	20	21	22	23	24	25
26	27	28	29	30		

This month marks the 10th anniversary of the planting of the first large palm at Palm Lake Beachmere Sands. Palm Lake Resorts landscapers brought it in by truck and lowered the tree into the ground by crane, causing quite a buzz amongst residents.

Qld School Holidays   Public Holidays   Qld /Brisbane

Appointments

This month's memories

May

Sun	Mon	Tues	Wed	Thurs	Fri	Sat
					1	2
3	LABOUR DAY 4	5	6	7	8	9
10	11	12	13	14	15	16
17	18	19	20	21	22	23
24	25	26	27	28	29	30
31						

May is the start of our glorious sunsets.

As the summer comes to an end and we head into winter they become more and more vibrant - deep red, orange and gold.

Qld School Holidays *Public Holidays* *Qld /Brisbane*

Appointments

_____
_____
_____
_____
_____
_____
_____
_____
_____
_____
_____
_____
_____
_____
_____
_____
_____ -
_____

This month's memories

_____
_____
_____
_____
_____
_____
_____
_____
_____
_____
_____
_____
_____
_____
_____
_____
_____
_____
_____

June

Sun	Mon	Tues	Wed	Thurs	Fri	Sat
	1	2	3	4	5	6
7	8	9	10	11	12	13
14	15	16	17	18	19	20
WINTER SOLSTICE 21	22	23	24	25	26	27
28	29	30				

June is pruning time in Beachmere. Prune roses within 6 weeks of the Winter Solstice. Before the end of July, prune spring-flowering and spring-fruiting plants, fruit trees, including apples, pears figs and olives and ornamental grasses.

Qld School Holidays

Public Holidays

Qld /Brisbane

Appointments

_____
_____
_____
_____
_____
_____
_____
_____
_____
_____
_____
_____
_____
_____
_____
_____ -
_____

This month's memories

_____
_____
_____
_____
_____
_____
_____
_____
_____
_____
_____
_____
_____
_____
_____
_____
_____

July

Sun	Mon	Tues	Wed	Thurs	Fri	Sat
			1	2	3	4
5	6	7	8	9	10	11
12	13	14	15	16	17	18
19	20	21	22	23	24	25
26	27	28	29	30	31	

It's strawberry time! Local farms are in full swing in July. In the fields around Beachmere, pickers on their little green trolleys are hard at work among the rows. Canny locals know when to turn up and "Pick Your Own" and jam makers look for "seconds" bargains.

Qld School Holidays   Public Holidays   Qld /Brisbane

Appointments

_____
_____
_____
_____
_____
_____
_____
_____
_____
_____
_____
_____
_____
_____
_____
_____ -

This month's memories

_____
_____
_____
_____
_____
_____
_____
_____
_____
_____
_____
_____
_____
_____
_____
_____

August

Sun	Mon	Tues	Wed	Thurs	Fri	Sat
						1
2	3	4	5	6	7	8
9	10	11	**Ekka Day** 12	13	14	15
16	17	18	19	20	21	22
23	24	25	26	27	28	29
30	31					

Winter is drawing to a close. It's EKKA time in Brisbane and family time for purple swamp hens in Beachmere. Any time between June and November swamp hens can be seen leading a troop of little black chicks from the waterholes to graze. Check the nets on your veggie patches - swamp hens love seedlings!

Qld School Holidays   Public Holidays   Qld /Brisbane

Appointments

_____
_____
_____
_____
_____
_____
_____
_____
_____
_____
_____
_____
_____
_____
_____
_____
_____
_____
_____ -

This month's memories

_____
_____
_____
_____
_____
_____
_____
_____
_____
_____
_____
_____
_____
_____
_____
_____
_____
_____
_____

September

Sun	Mon	Tues	Wed	Thurs	Fri	Sat
		1	2	3	4	5
6	7	8	9	10	11	12
13	14	15	16	17	18	19
20	21	22	23	24	25	26
27	28	29	30			

Spring has sprung. The roses are throwing their new shoots, fruit is blossoming and the nights are still crisp and clear. At full moon, Beachmere nights are as bright as day and an evening walk along the beach is quite magical.

Qld School Holidays   Public Holidays   Qld /Brisbane

Appointments

_____
_____
_____
_____
_____
_____
_____
_____
_____
_____
_____
_____
_____
_____
_____
_____
_____

This month's memories

_____
_____
_____
_____
_____
_____
_____
_____
_____
_____
_____
_____
_____
_____
_____
_____
_____

October

Sun	Mon	Tues	Wed	Thurs	Fri	Sat
				1	2	3
4	**KING'S BIRTHDAY** 5	6	7	8	9	10
11	12	13	14	15	16	17
18	19	20	21	22	23	24
25	26	27	28	29	30	31

October is the start of storm season. Time to make sure your home and garden are ready for strong winds and heavy rain. Luckily, we are spared many of the worst storms as the "Beachmere Dome" sends them north and south to bother Redcliffe and the Sunshine Coast.

Qld School Holidays   *Public Holidays*   *Qld /Brisbane*

Appointments

_____
_____
_____
_____
_____
_____
_____
_____
_____
_____
_____
_____
_____
_____
_____
_____
_____ -
_____

This month's memories

_____
_____
_____
_____
_____
_____
_____
_____
_____
_____
_____
_____
_____
_____
_____
_____
_____
_____
_____
_____
_____

November

Sun	Mon	Tues	Wed	Thurs	Fri	Sat
1	2	3	4	5	6	7
8	9	10	11	12	13	14
15	16	17	18	19	20	21
22	23	24	25	26	27	28
29	30					

On a day in November, no one can predict which day, clouds of butterflies emerge from the bush and flutter through our gardens looking for nectar and somewhere to lay their eggs. So soft and lovely, most of us don't mind a few caterpillars later in summer, and the birds deal with most of them anyway.

Qld School Holidays   Public Holidays   Qld /Brisbane

Appointments

_____
_____
_____
_____
_____
_____
_____
_____
_____
_____
_____
_____
_____
_____
_____
_____

This month's memories

_____
_____
_____
_____
_____
_____
_____
_____
_____
_____
_____
_____
_____
_____
_____
_____

December

Sun	Mon	Tues	Wed	Thurs	Fri	Sat
			1	2	3	4	5
6	7	8	9	10	11	12
13	14	15	16	17	18	19
20	21	22	23	Xmas Eve 24	Xmas Day 25	Boxing Day 26
27	28	29	30	New Year's Eve 31		

"Dear Santa, I've been a very good boy this year... mostly. Especially near the shiny ornaments. And Mum and Dad have been good too."

Christmas is a day of love and traditions, a special day spent in the warm circle of family and friends, including the furry ones.

Qld School Holidays   Public Holidays   Qld /Brisbane

Appointments

_____

_____

_____

_____

_____

_____

_____

_____

_____

_____

_____

_____

_____

_____

_____

_____

_____

_____

This month's memories

_____

_____

_____

_____

_____

_____

_____

_____

_____

_____

_____

_____

_____

_____

_____

_____

_____

_____

Phone Numbers

Name

Number

Phone Numbers

Name

Number

Emails

Name

Email Address

Emails

Name	Email Address
_____	_____
_____	_____
_____	_____
_____	_____
_____	_____
_____	_____
_____	_____
_____	_____
_____	_____
_____	_____
_____	_____
_____	_____
_____	_____
_____	_____
_____	_____
_____	_____
_____	_____
_____	_____
_____	

Record your best memory of 2026

_____

_____

_____

_____

_____

_____

_____

_____

_____

_____

_____

_____

_____